Circuitous Course:

A Co-Created Life

Gregory A. Kompes

Fabulist Flash Publishing
Las Vegas, NV

ISBN: 978-0-9793612-9-6

Fabulist Flash Publishing

PO Box 570368

Las Vegas, Nevada, 89157

Dedication

To All the Co-Creators in my life...

   ...you may or may not know who you are

Table of Contents

Circuitous Course:

A Co-Created Life

Gregory A. Kompes

Circuitous Course

I strolled along your craggy shore
Searched for shells, learned lore
Waves crashed, suns rose high
With every breath, I longed to soar

I danced in puddles with friends at the fair
Home for rainy weeks, deluge of time to spare
Fell in love and out, celebrated romance
The remembrance of them my only souvenir

I witnessed as close as anyone might
Rushing waters, illustrious falls, inspirational rites
Flood never ceasing, encounters teamed, splashed
Yet, no mementos remain, except memory's sprite

I ascended the summit into cathedral domes
Traversed underground crypts, stately homes
Great museums admired; countryside navigated
Wish more'd been captured in paint, pixels, or tomes

I read great books, sang masters' songs
Believed in gods, performed for throngs
Published a few words, hoping they mattered
Always expecting more, my beating heart longs

I traveled the world, experience my wake
Loved, lost, won, knew hate; been original, fake
Sold, bartered, stole, gave; what a circuitous course
Like others before, fading memories my only keepsake

Dreams

From here to
Eternity, from
Sea to mountain peak,
Life not dreamed
Ends quiet.

Noise and notice
Hither and yon
Determine how
Life becomes.
Unquiet

We dream, we
Hope, it's what
We do. We
Believe
as we can.

Yet, somehow,
Someday, without
Dreams we become and
Forget that we are

Us, not another's
Folly. No matter what
Your goal. No matter your

Dreams. Folly if others
Decide your
Consequence.

Yours are
Dreams
To trumpet as you wish, to
Follow as you dare, to
Become you.

Silent noise

Silent noise	I trust with faith;
To me,	They encourage.
Knowing,	It's what they do.
At sleepy day's start;	Drive on, flourish
Loneliness ends, for	Somewhere, first black
During that light,	Crystal, now blue.
For me, an old friend.	Travels my Journey
Silence awakes,	Through time,
My mind opens,	Voices lead.
And then.	Willed or divine?
A channel through	This darkness, now
darkness,	lightened
No apologies or amends.	Silence, reverberates
Toward voices,	With visions of time
Unceasing, incessant,	Noise
Believing, in essence	Out of sync
Those hours theirs'.	Silence enlightened.

We Tamburitzans

Each pluck of the pick
Every costume flair
Magic built
In the air.

We children sang, danced
With gusto and might
Our music wafted
Into the night.

We traveled the world
Or so it seemed
To us who plucked
Twirled, and preened.

Those times are gone
The stage is bare.
Memories only now,
For those who were there.

Now Split and Mostar
All Yugoslavia changed,
Dubrovnik, Sarajevo,
And Zagreb divided.

Retained memories linger
For the future some must
Lest the magic be lost
And return to the dust.

Gregory A. Kompes

Shifting Sand

Ideas through space
Shifting sublime
We move the world
By grains, through time.

One moment, dunes,
Sandscapes created.
Shift one spot,
Another, eliminated.

What's left? Now right
At center, above,
Forward, below,
Beyond, true love.

We sift, we shovel
Lift, move;
Shuttle, accept,
Discard, remove.

Add heat, pressure,
Some light and some time.
Desire, empathy,
Maybe some rhyme.

Realization: It's our
Never ending quest.
We must move mountains
Before we rest.

Gregory A. Kompes

Blue Glass and Butterflies

I had a desire
The quiver flew
It came back quickly;
I found it in blue.

I had a want
Little at first
It came back quickly;
Quenched my thirst.

An attraction came next,
How could it not?
A piece here, a bit there
Tied in a knot.

Yet as they came
Wants, desires, attractions
New perspectives arrive
Position, no traction.

Will this never end,
This quest, these desires?
Will life stay driven
Toward something red, with tires?

Our universe thrives
From hope and extension,
We flourish and prosper
Joy fuels expansion.

Gregory A. Kompes

The Weaver

The Weaver weaves thread by thread
Slowly shuttles under over on end
Until together and intertwined
Intended pattern revealed.

The Weaver unweaves then thread by thread
The labored form deconstructed.
A new color is found, a new design desired;
Unused threads dropped underfoot.

The Weaver now weaves, once again
Some old with the new, reconstruction
Until in the doing, intention created
Surpassing the first, the second, the third...

More new threads discovered, new colors dyed
Another pass through forward behind
Threads then pulled, scattered, inserted
Those not reused remain discarded.

Responsibility unending, task eternal
Yet, the Weaver weaves knowing
Results aren't the goal
Instead, life's action driven.

Père Lachaise

Rain falls, soft, light
Dampening paths where
Famous bodies rest,

Leaves gone,
Branches exposed
Like souls

Monuments crumbled.
Only rubble, rocks,
A single rose

Time marked
By footsteps along
Wet trails, paths

Debris, now snapshots
Writers, painters, artists
Extraordinary, sublime

These dead in Paris
Honored with tombs,
Fallen among the rest

Crumbled lives
Never to be again
Scattered like leaves.

Gregory A. Kompes

New beginnings and ends

Everything calm,
No pall, no din
For the world to see
New beginnings and ends

We wait, breath baited
Action, reaction recorded
Change will come
New beginnings and ends

There's precedent, experience
We've seen this before
Different, but same
New beginnings and ends

A circle of life,
Maybe or no
A cycle perhaps
New beginnings and ends

It simply continues
Whether liked or not
We along for the ride
New beginnings and ends

One thing is certain
No fact denied
Change provides contrast
New beginnings and ends.

Le Louvre

Famous creations mass sought:
Smiling Mona, under glass,
Aphrodite holds nothing.

Corridors travelled; Gallery stops
Masters hung silent, some
Vibrant, others revered.

Sculptors, painters, crafters most,
Metal, wood, rock transformed;
Marbled hall stockrooms.

Miles walked, seems true
Catacombed works trapped
Inside venerated walls.

Time Dulled; Age cracked
Still lives, dead royalty
Withered fruit, forgotten lands.

Forward movement, through
Time, space, where
Colored shapes burst forth

The Slave enchained remains,
Medusa's Raft raptured chaos,
Winged Victory guides nothing.

Questions abound; No meaning given

Knowledge lacked; Maybe none needed.

Admiration required to proceed.

Ceded Life
...for Chris

Rocks emerge at water's edge.
Annals scoring winds,
Searing days, tumultuous seas.
History sculpted crags.

Seasons pass, regress
Ocean waves chisel,
Undulate, swell, surge.
Lapsed time fades.

Cold and heat chip change.
Each spell transforms, amends.
Differences appear, subtle;
Extreme over eons.

Lives the same lived.
If deeper delved, still
Fight and fortune, this one filled
Evolution's forced return

Destiny Decided

Destiny decided
Can't get it wrong
Travel through eternity
Can't get it done

Transitions

Boyhood winters
On a frozen lake,
Jump from cliffs;
Dream of escape.

Transitions,
Like clockwork thrive,
Create worlds,
Alter lives.

Long beach walks
With lanky boys
Juvenile sex
Higher stakes

Transitions,
Like clockwork thrive,
Create worlds,
Alter lives.

Young men now
Drink and smoke in bars,
Laugh through life;
Stay alive.

Transitions,
Like clockwork thrive,
Create worlds,
Alter lives.

Gregory A. Kompes

Settled adults,
Jobs and mortgages,
Dreams of bars,
Beaches and cliffs.

Transitions,
Like clockwork thrive,
Create worlds,
Alter lives.

Joy

Review of racks, grey shirt select, grey slacks,
grey shoes? No, black.
Survey, grey. Replace with another shade today.

Grey cat purrs, curled.
Examine. Replace. Add socks.
Argyle, grey and black. Belt.

Explanation? No. One no one deserved.
Today; like others, grey.
Began. Progressed. One moment, next.

Would there be color, other? Unknown.
Cat blue to red moves. Purrs. Sheds.
Trousers, shirt. Lint brush scanned.

Tie? No. None to impress, today.
Check shoes. Shined. On. Laces tied.
Why prepare? Go where? Out,

Any place, away, one grey to another
Hope eternal, colors return.
Sun dappled path. Leaves, branches breeze brushed.

Patterns shift, change,
Ahead, leaves dusty;
Illuminate sidewalk patched; elucidate grey mood.

Gregory A. Kompes

One yellow glow. A mirage? No.
Amble ahead, gait stilted. Clouds pass,
Blocked sun emerges at canopied conduit's end.

Arrival water. Not the objective, end.
Ocean gentle, not glass, calm.
Bench at the edge invites; receives.

Sky skimming gulls, lighting from black,
Fish catches, grey scales, hidden sunlight sparkles,
Hints of gold reflect.

Grey ash drops, cigarette to trousers grey.
Dust away. Reprimand, internal.
Gull approaches, sea piling perch extends,

Remnant of time, dock, perhaps, or pier.
Calls to no one. Waits. Takes flight,
Upheaval. Descends.

Pelican, pole roosts on paddle feet.
Long bill. Long neck. Large body, grey.
Grey eyes each. Comment tacit.

Again, ash on slacks. Reprimand repeat.
Sun ratchets notch by notch, horizon closer ticks.
End of its, his day. Demise scrutinized.

Fate accept.
In that moment, orb between disappearance final,
Black night emerge, please.

Water shifts, deep and solid.
Grass glimmers, its own shade, different, subtle.
Skies open, contents spill, surface.

Wind. Dust of time takes flight, settles
Consumes.
Moment, flash, everything as it should,

Grey companion escapes, takes flight.
Rain cleaned, green, tree's leaves dance.
Flowers glow shades of red and blue.

Day, dust drenched, water soaked, now fresh.
Reemergence, a Technicolor world.
Moment pure, before heat, cleansing.

Placation. Deep breath, even air
Reassures, green taste. For time first,
Head to sky, pelted,

Closed eyes, consonance…joy.

Gregory A. Kompes

Transitions

Tarnished, tired, showing age-old ware
Realization, the result of living.
Advancement in time, in place
Nub of a life, worth living?
Swap, replace, change occasion, location,
Importance of this life worth living.
Terminate this, go for unsullied
Interpret a new beginning.
Original ideas, no such thing
New, with sparkle, all the same
Swerve to the subsequent experience.

We Will Return

... for Todd

Dropped, middle of nowhere,
Drinking grapes, sunshine basking.
Sculpture surrounds, Bernini's Horses
Students emerge from shallow water.
Smiles honest, amazement sincere,
Time of your life, eh kid?

Dropped, middle of nowhere,
Another dumb church
Coin dropped in. Lights rise.
Scenes ablaze under century's dirt.
Time of your life, eh kid?

Dropped, middle of nowhere,
Gladiators triumphed, now collapsing.
Elephants, ships, thumps up, thumbs down
Stones overturned, decommissioned, reused.
Time of your life, eh kid?

Dropped, middle of nowhere,
We look, we find. Stairs rise. Cameras snap.
We climb, we sit, we climb, we sit.
No view, just stairs, filled with lunchers
Time of your life, eh kid?

Dropped, middle of nowhere,
More Bernini, small bees buzz.
Neighborhood scene, only us
For this we came?
Time of your life, eh kid?

Dropped, middle of somewhere,
More horses emerge, Salvi's waters glisten.
Backs turn. Coins tossed. Cameras snap.
Another toss, not for effect.
Time of your life, eh kid?

Gregory A. Kompes

The Only Two

First romance, handheld tour through
Verdant earth, Spring's soaked ground
Life explodes, tall tree canopies shade.
What lies in these daylight shadows?
Ferns engulf, ivy crawls, birds call, answer.

Hands held tighter, laughter, amazement
Seasonal transformation
Creek turns river, deluged bridge damp.
What lies in these daylight shadows?
Over, beyond, we seek the place

Through those trees, over that path
Traveled before, alone, always
Alone in solace, in peace, in time.
What lies in these daylight shadows?
Now together, that someone.

Ramble through brambles. Really?
Yes. It's there. First promise.
Pricker plants trap, surround, swallow.
What lies in these daylight shadows?
No fear, excitement.

Lush valley spreads below, point, lookout
Favorite spot. Before alone, now with another.
Flowers in bloom perfume the air.
What lies in these daylight shadows?
A kiss.

Visions from a Distance

While spending time with my team today,
I was taken back to that place,
just beyond the line.

I was shown many different universes—
separate from our own never ending universe,
spreading out in all directions, in all shapes, sizes, colors.

All with their own inhabitants
enjoying their own concepts of time and space.
Some the same as ours, some different.

None crossing over with any other.
Each place, as its own, independent creation.
So very cool!

And, they took me further,
and all of those entity universes became single little pricks of
light,
rather like we see our own stars.

Gregory A. Kompes

University Circle Saturdays

Travel alone, a place of adulthood
Hit the pothole, just for fun.
Students with books, lessons, instructors

Sound surrounds my yellow bass
From each hall and room left, center, right,
Tympani tune, boom on cue

Ahead, cellos swoon, bows high in the air
Brass blares while strings shimmer
Pages turn, rests counted, bottom applied.

Over our heads, his arms indicate
"It's a comic opera, the music shouldn't be funny."
Temperaments of all sizes flare.

Guiding the troop, we follow as we can.
Years of Ginistera, Bach, Brahms, Rossini
Concerti, symphonies, overtures, andante.

Lead, we follow, waiting for breaks
Smoking together in plastic-chaired halls.
Children as adults, all for different reasons.

Pressed white shirts and trousers mark seasons' passages,
Most parents attend concerts
Following progress, congratulating themselves.

Searching the crowd, Others' parents provide
Praise and pats that I enjoy.
Just another University Circle Saturday, alone.

Our Journey

Energy shifts as our lives align
Outcomes and results are lovely, sublime
Parallel worlds move forward as we sow
Vineyards incubate, flourish and grow;
Cooperative plot tended, yet mine.

Throughout our voyage we drink the wine
Tasting our share offered from the divine.
Our journey traversed, joy plus woe
Energy shifts as our lives align.

When we depart, shrouded in lime
Corporal shell smashed, mirrors decline
As energy and soul, we travel, flow
Outside, beyond physical, this we know
Yet, we too, like you, live on through time
Tending the garden, expanded design.
Energy shifts as our lives align.

Gregory A. Kompes

We Knew We'd Be In Love Forever

Elephant ears, mustarded corn dogs
Midway games, friends, laughter, fun.
Holding hands near blue ribbon hogs
Arms wrapped, talked for hours into her up knot.
We knew we'd be in love forever.

The Ferris Wheel, Tilt 'o Whirl
Scrambler crush, State Fair fun.
Long kisses beneath banners unfurled;
Petting the bear for her I won.
We knew we'd be in love forever.

We worked our shifts; hours turned days,
Days turned weeks, our summer passed.
Juried halls of quilts, pies, jams, quite an array;
Expressed moments of love, at long last.
We knew we'd be in love forever.

Summer ended, as summers will,
We returned to our homes,
The insurmountable distance filled
With love letter tomes.
We knew we'd be in love forever.

With expressions beyond our age and passion
We attempt to prolong our brief infatuation.
Within a few months our love fell out of fashion
Yet our experience taught that love can and will happen.
We knew we'd be in love forever.

Winesap Apples

Autumn leaves descend
Red, gold, yellow, brown
Establish drifts that foreshadow
Along hilly country roads.

Humid summer ended
Sweater weather begun
Our annual fall pilgrimage
We embark, apple bound.

Through harvest cut fields
Corn, wheat, pumpkin for pies
We witness delighted
The season's passing.

We travel with speed
Stomachs lift and fall
Like the drifted leaves
Flurry, take flight, resettle.

Visitation stop, familial graves
Roadside-stand purchased
Autumnal bouquets placed.
Left to mark time at All Saints.

Memorial complete.
Life again lived, persist
Deeper into Chardon's hills
Toward Sage's Farm we thread.

Gregory A. Kompes

The smell of apples draws us.
Well-sacked, cider-pressed;
Cheese, honey, candy arrayed
A rite of passage at fall's shrine.

Homeward bound now
Back to city streets, cottage homes,
While we snack on reaped treasures
The season's harvest sown.

Star Light, Star Bright

Direction alteration
Quick modification
Path transformation
Vague variation

Present creation
Only reaction
Past action
Only distraction

Future aspiration
Foremost illumination
Another day's creation
Tomorrow's deviation

Gregory A. Kompes

Heidelberg

Off to sleepy Tiffin's side
Welcome, yet unwanted
Stone walls, ivy covered
Manicured lawns, Tree dotted

Moving through time
Freshman at King,
Junior at Willard toward
Self-realized sexual exile.

Bridge thrown pennies:
Kiss received;
Caution thrown windward,
Kiss offered, rejected, received.

Friends made, kept, lost,
Forgotten, remembered.
Kopper Kettle road trips,
Joy of youth, pain of growth

Discovered Schumann, Schoenberg,
Copland.
Survived with Stein, Steinbeck,
Mozart.

Embraced Mann as God
It was required.

Retreated from Mann,
Human, flawed.

Embraced Bevelander.
It was desired.
Embraced Pepper.
Almost got me through.

Tours to nowhere,
Rules followed, broken
Regimen to somewhere,
Rules broken, heart followed.

No degree held harbor;
Escape to freedom from
Hallowed halls; self-educated
Journey preferred, continued.

Maple Stir

Chill in the air
Snow barely gone
Up through the boughs
Sap rises

Roofed buckets
Tap attached to capture
Liquid through its daily
Rise and fall

Clean, nearly clear
Smokehouse destined
Fire boiled smoke
Scents the air

Syrup for pancakes
Candy for sucking
Least known
Maple Stirs

The liquid hot,
The stick small
Motion fast round
The bowl

End result a cross
Between liquid and solid
A sweet delight
Of the late winter season.

Sarasota

Balmy nights, sun drenched days
Random escape to personal freedom
Pit orchestra nights, rehearsal days
Entry to adulthood Sarasota style.

Railroad flat, hardwood floors
Comfortable porch, afternoon rains
Rent to pay, Cat to feed
Hundred year live oak

Out of the closet, into the theatres
Sarasota hired for years: Studio,
Asolo, Friends, Apple, Players
Hand-to-mouth life, appreciated

Happy Hour cocktail friendships
Moonlit dolphin walks
Fleeting love, naked beaches
Sandy blankets, passionate embraces

Coming of age without reason
Instead through trial and error
Infatuation, angst, optimism, fear
Freedom a choice, rite of passage

Art conformed, payment due
Freedom turned obligation
Unready for compromise
Back in the Ford toward a new location.

Chattering

The gold globe lies heavy over the sea.
Small waves shimmer, sparkle,
Touched here with green, there with gold,
Beneath, behind, and below Kingfisher blue tones.

In the distance, up the shore, on the breeze,
A couple's laughter grazes the sands.
Small birds at water's edge lift in gentle flight.
They circle, observe, land again where they started,
Choosing small fish from the pools of tide, chattering.

Beauty. Color. Light. These are the things of life.
Fame. Fortune. Success. These are the goals.
We see the world from a dissident light.
So, we don't agree, Paul?

No, Frank. We see the world from divergent perspectives.
We dream distinctive futures.
Yet, we respect each other.
The two looked into the eyes of the other, smiling a devoted
smile.
I raise my glass to you Frank, my friend.
And, I you.

The deep red wine glimmers through raised crystal, eyes
focused.

Gregory A. Kompes

The colors shift again,
Redder now, more sallow
The heavy orange orb drops lower.
Laughter returns; no distant birds rise.

Bach. Mozart. Handel. Pachelbel. These provide proof of
order.
Debussy. Cage. Schoenberg. Bevelander. Chaos proves there
is no order.
We attend the universe with different ears.
Yet, we're deaf to each other, Paul?
No, Frank. We perceive the customary on discordant waves.
We long for alternate pasts.
However, we harmonize together.
The two breathed as one, a seductive breath.
I hear you Frank, my friend.
And, I you.

The needle skips, static crackles, longing silent.

Darkness creeps until the switch is flipped,
Day extinguished.
With vision blinded, sound amplifies.
The couple is gone now.
Up the shore? Indoors? Into the sea?

Michelangelo. Raphael. Titian. Leonardo.
Johns. Warhol. Brueghel. Picasso...Me.
You? Who has added you to any list yet?

40

Gregory A. Kompes

I. We add ourselves to this list. Leaving judgment of
ourselves to others is folly.
So, we dissent, Paul?
No, Frank. We layer disputed options, yet long for affable
times.
Alas, we find them together.
Their misty eyes smile through sorrow.
Paul reaches for Frank's soft hand, my friend.
Frank places his own upon the top, and I yours.

The candle silenced by a breeze from the sea, auricles strain.
More wine arrives.

The moon, high in the night sky,
Lights water, glows.
Gentle waves kiss the shore
Calming breezes settle the day.
A couple's whispers nudge the night; their steps avoid the
rising tide.

Confucius. Seneca. Aquinas. Hume...Me.
Lucretius. Pascal. Spinoza. Leibnitz.
Not you? You haven't added yourself to this list?
I? We don't add ourselves to this list.
So, we agree to disagree, Paul?
No, Frank. We disagree to aggrieve.
But, we're discordant together.
The two frown through snaps of flame.

Paul's smoke swirls into the night's stillness, my friend?
Frank watches their smoke intertwine. Yes, and I yours.

The tree has fallen, has anyone heard, silent searching for
meaning.

Darkness fades,
The glow arrives,
The tide subsides.
A new dawn pauses, granting a final moment's respite.
Where's the couple now?

Success. Fame. Fortune. These are the things of life.
Art. Beauty. Color. Light. These are the goals.
We see the world from an incongruous plane.
So, we don't agree, Paul?
No, Frank. We see the world from disentangled
perspectives. We dream for the sake of dreaming.
Finally, we complement each other.
The two looked, eyes smiling a loving smile.
I raise my brushes to you Frank, my friend.
And I, my quill to you.

The morning rays blast through leaded glass; prisms dance
to the sound of the waves; eyes focus on the days' work.

They approach from opposite ends of the sand,
Notice each other, pause with a smile, a kind word.
They walk up the shore together,
Collecting shells, laughing.
Birds take flight.
They circle, observe, land again further up the shore,
Chattering.

River Sestina

Raging waters, white capped churn
Roaring river from which we learn
We expend our energy on the rushing stream
When we head our boat in the other extreme
Choose we must, to travel up or down
Each moment of our joyous life

Direction matters little in this life
The goal simply stated: experience the churn
When we head with the flow, travel down
The river, our movements fast as we learn
Our journey becomes harder, pain extreme
When we choose, to head up the stream

When we choose to point our boat upstream
The work becomes a difficult task of life
The battle to move our boat, extreme
As we head up directly into the churn
Yet even on this errand, still we learn
The journey's just harder up than down

It's our choice, head up or down
Go with the current or against the stream
The results the same, we grow we learn
But upstream battle creates a harder life
The efforts greater with every rushing churn
The oars in hand make for tired arms, extreme

Gregory A. Kompes

How simple it is to reach the extreme
How simple it is to point the boat down
How simple it is to enjoy the frothy churn
How simple it is to travel the stream
How simple it is to love this life
How simple it is to experience and learn

If the physical existence we live leads us to learn
There is no venture too extreme
Filling with love our hearts and life
When our boat is directed stream-word down
When we enjoy the journey on our stream
Cherish the moments of the river's churn

Who Questions Now?

A generation questioned, most survived
Now in charge they forge the same rhetoric
That led them to question the elders before them.

Fewer question now, and those so quietly.
No return to the Magic Dragon's haze and
Purple Rain utopia of psychedelic times.

Wars continue on humanity and the same
Drugs that brought questions into light.
Yet, somehow, now, more drugged than ever

None question in ways or methods that
Get the originators, now leaders, to take
Notice of anything beyond their personal

Message of greed and power. So the circle
Spins and expands. New generations quieter
In their questioning style. If at all. Yet more drugs

Flow than ever before. Numbing down the electorate
And their rhetoric. The hate mongers continue to spew
As before, yet their voices are louder than the quiet
protests.

Freedom and power remain within the old framework.
Self against self against those who label others non-patriot.
Yet, self into self we continue to challenge quietly by living a

Life worth living.

Gregory A. Kompes

Thanks, Kate

Energy pulses, day, night
Through grimy gridded
Traffic-filled streets

Midtown home, three flights walk
Above the Jewish bakery
Neighbors to cheap Chinese

Across Ninth Avenue
Neon Emergency
Illuminates corner fruit

Window view
Future hopes cast
Toward Broadway

Summer lumbers
No relief through
Open air-shaft windows

Awaiting *The Break*
City goal: escape
To the road

Life off the rack
Office temp jobs
Ill-fitting jackets

Months pass
Hopes diminish
Finally the call

Bus & Truck replaces
Apartment share
Life on the Road

Not 'til September
Roommate reprieve
Three more weeks

Route 1 & 1A

Snow falling heavily
Fueling my desire
Three travel days lost
In front of a friend's fire

I dreamed as I waited
Of my travels for fun
Destinations unknown
Views of sea, surf, sun

Finally the storm ceased
My departure permitted
Coastal points north
That's where I headed

A mighty goal: Explore
Maine's inlets and shores
Portland to Campobello
Only one day now, not four

Sea blue waters
Skies a lighter shade
Route 1 and 1a
Before me lay

Coastal inlet lighthouses
Grey craggy shores
Ice-burdened lobster traps
Roads snow adorned

Gregory A. Kompes

Anonymous motorist
Navigate, explore
Time meaningless until
The view sunset obscured

In the darkness, to Bangor
I made my way
Spring Break was ending
The very next day

Feeling Lost

Feeling lost, where to turn
Ideas abound, dissatisfy

Feeling lost, anywhere to turn
Choices abound, inspiration

Feeling lost, nowhere to turn
Mistakes abound, chastisement

Feeling lost, somewhere to turn
Indecisions abound, running away

Feeling lost, turn wherever
Thoughts abound, action none

Feeling lost, whatever thought
Ideas abound, dreams

Feeling lost, everywhere searched
Nothing new presents itself

Feeling lost, where
Something new awaits

Uncolored Discoveries

Unconnected
Self, spirit, soul

Searching wide paths
Journey with heartfelt hope

Desires chime, call, yet
Answers, discoveries, uncolored

Weed wandering
Awaiting inspiration, direction

Exploring mountain treks, yet
Questions flourish, fear grows

Yearning peals, beckons
Expedition, heartbreak unending

Separated, independent
Ideas flow, latch upon nothing

Panoramic views, visions
Voices clamor, Hear Us!

Ascertaining truth, trust, optimism
Clinging faith, anticipation

All Hollows Even

O, mysterious night, veil lifts
Shifts between Dark and Light

Black cats welcome, play, purr, howl
Dead friends, relatives returned to prowl

Stingy Jack, denied Heaven and Hell
Follows Satan's ember in a turnip's shell

Children then with soul cakes rewarded
Prayers exchanged for the dearly departed

Pray for the dead, if you must
See into a future that is just

Apples pealed before candlelit mirror
Her future husband she hopes will appear

First to bite into fruit bobbing
Is first to marry, seconds sobbing

Sleepy Hollow's Headless Horsemen rides
Blazing pumpkin eyes glare as he strides

Costume clad Children holler Trick or Treat
Hoping for a Snickers to unwrap and eat.

My Snowman

Yuletide carols play. Scratchy records
Compete with hi-fi static, livid words.
Tree in stand, more effort than joy
Parent's control competition keen.

Lights next, string after string
Arduous chore, or so *he* says.
Dark made light. We anticipate.
Boxes of ornaments, our task, await.

Finally their time, tissue-wrapped
History emerges once again
After a year of slumber in
Hidden attic peak safety.

Drunk father, angry mother
Opposite corners revisited.
Their fury unimportant as snow
Flies beyond ice-frosted windows.

Memories we hang, gently as directed.
Fragile testimony in glass and ceramic
Proof of times past, happier, or so *she* says.
Remembrance fills the fragrant spaces.

There it is, finally emerged from the morass
The shiny snowman, my favorite, at last.
Blue and gold sparkle, his smile sincere
He follows our progress year after year.

Gregory A. Kompes

I linger a moment, my friend in hand
Perfect spot chosen for his holiday to spend.
He'll keep watch over me from evergreen perch
Through holiday storms and holiday mirth.

Last task reached, place tinsel,
Strand by strand, on command. Yet,
Christmas hope survives. My snowman
Preserves and restores magic each season.

Winter Solstice Haiku

An instant in time
The longest night of the year
Brings holiday cheer

Gregory A. Kompes

Winter Solstice

An instant in time, that longest night
Astronomical, symbolic, ritualistic

Orion's stars dance, his belt twinkles
Returned again, our season's sky guide

Some starve, others gorge
This merriest season

We travel all, aware or not
Past and beyond toward the future

Journey toward renewal
We skyward watch with hope

Stonehenge Haiku

Great temple of stone
Dot on the English landscape
Ancient mystery

Ancient Rock

Drums beat, flutes haunt
Quartzsite anticipation

Dusty lots, paths
Ancient rocks astound

Not what expected
Exactly what expected

They call from booths, tables
Magic abounds all around

Ancients arise, rediscovered
Universe creations, phenomenon

Geodes cut, uncut
Salt lights, healing stones

Moroccan Fossil selected
Madagascar Quartz acquired

New experience
Old Friends found

Energy lifted, vibration high
All the way home, beyond

Summer Sense

Freshly tarred school roof
Summer pronouncement

Lazy afternoons, Marlboro
Smoke weaving through
green-leafed trees

Freedom bound on generationally
Shared bikes, soar—hands air raised

Fish-fouled rolling waves
Erie's waters smash against
Time-worn wooden pier

Open doors/windows day/night
Small town trust, safety known

Rolling thunder announces
Lightning tainted, tornado
Dotted black skies

Ants scour blades of grass
Cicadas hum their summer song

Tomatoes flourish, Corn skyward
Dollar in the coffee can to feed from
Roadside farm stands along rolled hills

Cool mornings/muggy afternoons
Fresh cut grass, streetlight timers

Wire-perched birds, sunsets glorious
Solitude/friendship/potato salad
Tag, you're always it

Classroom lists = summer's death knoll
Capture lightning bugs one last time

Summer Breeze

afternoon heat: Trees droop
no Breeze stirs
distant Sky blackens

lone meadow Horse, tail thwaps
biting Flies off Hide
no Breeze agitates

pair of Dogs porch laze
dream Rabbits chased
no Bark required

darkened Clouds approach
yet, no Breeze disturbs
passing Ants' progress

rusted Sign falls, finally
strange, no Breeze troubled
single Dog-eye opened, closed

sudden darkness, Sun blocked
stray Cicada hums, anticipation
quiet Breeze encouraged

deceitful Clouds progress
another Day, perhaps
today, no Breeze consoles

Singing Crystal

Fee paid, enter crowded space
Floor position selected
Anticipation builds

Lay back, relax, feel
Deep bass vibrations, head echoes
Quiet mind attained

Body trembles, lightly
Tones change, alto over drone
Past memories emerge

Pulsation, throbbing tenor
Circles space, left, right, around
Heart opens, emotions flow

Air quivers, patterns emerge
Brief, fleeting thoughts, soprano
Recollected hurts released, healed

Bass, alto reverberations
Wobble air, movement, thoughts
Light flashes, auras resound

Soprano punctuation, tenor highs
Bing...Bong...Dong...mellow resonance
Thoughts still, nothing, blackness

Silenced internal vibrations
Resonate; Hour's journey complete
New peaceful existence begins.

Gregory A. Kompes

A Journeyman's Rondaeu

We join where two lonely roads meet.
Kindred spirits guided here, greet.
His nod tussles auburn hair 'round
Laughter, friendship, joy of sex found.
No thoughts, rumpled covers, love, heat.

Neither interested in girl's teats
We explore men for alternate treats.
We dance, we drink, spread love around
Where two lonely roads meet

Perfect moments merely a beat.
It matters not, sadly how sweet.
A journeyman's life again hounds
The road, she calls: come embrace sounds.
Travel further on; hope again beats
Where two lonely roads meet

Gregory A. Kompes

Summer's End

Hummingbirds air flight flower-focused dance
Dragon flies soaring in silent elance
Yellow billed Cuckoos foliage scuttle
Summer's conclusion, hurried yet subtle

Last run, shirtless ride, one more game of tag
Dark arrives earlier, bright streetlights nag
Lightning bugs glimmer, final heated night
Ultimate try to jump the besting height

Long pants, new shoes, outdoor playtime finished
My time to win summer's games diminished
Apples crisp, sunflowers bend, classroom now calls
Books to read, friends to make in hallowed halls

Eyes toward open windows drift, watch birds fly
Count the days 'till next year's fun, for now, sigh.

Gregory A. Kompes

Lunar Cycle

"Oh," you said when you bumped into me
Our eyes held that night, busy NYC corner
"In a hurry?" I asked. You: "No."
We drank until dawn
Under the new moon

Fresh experience, night after night
Movies, dinners, thunderstorm walks
Long conversations, shy kisses
As we explored Central Park
Under the waxing crescent moon

We waited, we agreed, it would mean more
Anticipation building about the first time
Scrabble, cards, hide 'n seek games
Sharing secrets, demons, dreams
Under the first quarter moon

Pinkies linked, I met your favorite art
Picasso, Pissarro, Rembrandt, Degas
Suits, ties, I introduced opera
Mozart, Rossini, Wagner, Strauss
Under the waxing gibbous moon

"It's time," you offered.
"I know," I lied.
What if after all this time

Gregory A. Kompes

We weren't compatible
Under the full moon

You spoke of rings, commitments
We found a new place to live
Not yours, not mine, but ours
George Washington Bridge view
Under the waning gibbous moon

I met your friends, you met mine
Everyone cordial, out of time
We wandered away from the party
To make love on the roof
Under the last quarter moon

You painted; I wrote
We made love
Our friends ignored us
Tickets purchased for Paris
Under the waning crescent moon

I arrived home with flowers
Our itinerary had arrived
I didn't see the note for hours
"Sorry, Love, just can't"
Under the dark moon

Thanksgiving Prayer

We gather together no matter the weather
This Fourth Thursday of November for
Turkey presented on Grandmother's platter

Each year we think: This time will be different
Hurts shall be forgotten, forgiven, bribed away
With overly sweet marshmallow-dotted potatoes

Yet, Long dead patriarchs claim preferences still
I've made his favorite again this year
Waldorf salad uneaten, no one liked it but him

Too much wine, not much cheer
Passed plates return heaped
Corn should heal their fears?

A heavy burden this table holds
Fights, anger, misunderstandings, affairs
Generational orphans hidden in Jell-O molds

Silence falls, going through the motions only
So much to consume, seconds anyone? he asks
Her truths doled out with great grandmother's stuffing

Children squirm as adults raise their voices
Scabs removed again to reveal so many unhealed wounds
Little ones forming mashed potato castles for protection

Too much said, but even more still to confess
Nothing will replace lost generations of dreams
While waiting for pumpkin pie, heaped with cream

Whose home are we at for Christmas?

Tour View

The bus pulled out
I waved good-bye
Headed out toward
The Great Divide.

First tour, first journey
Manifested request
We'd play the regions
At the producers behest

Musician services
Reaped little cash
I'd spend it all on
Booze, Sex, and hash

New audience each night
Different town every day
Afterward, we'd hit the clubs
Try to score or make hay

Miles flew by,
Days became weeks
Buses died,
Critics wept

Life had changed
Priorities, too
Morals were gone
Popularity grew

Gregory A. Kompes

Weeks turned to months
Night-time stranger's
Names forgotten
Signs of danger

Flash

Doors flash open
Shattered glass
Moonlight sparkle

Freedom moment
Slow motion
No one knows
Where I am

Flashbulbs pop
Old-fashioned thought
Twitter tweet

Fame precedes me
Fast forward
Everyone knows
Where I am

Obscurity sudden
No second birth
Dead phoenix

Sovereignty awarded
Stop motion
No one knows
Who I am

It's Christmas, recession be damned

Shiny paper, handmade bows
Presents piled high under the tree
Hopes, like sugarplums, dance

It's Christmas, recession be damned

Yet, we must wait, until all arrive
Family traveling from far and wide
Before a bow or paper scrap shredded

It's Christmas, downturn be damned

Not a rattle or shake of a single box
No detective work allowed
St. Nick's first impression preserved

It's Christmas, stagnation be damned

Snow falls heavy, blows, drifts
Frost forms firm in window corners
Yuletide log burns bright, warm

It's Christmas, decline be damned

Dad returns with Grandma
Cousins travel from frozen Heights
Foreign land Aunts arrive

It's Christmas, strike be damned

Gregory A. Kompes

Finally, everyone assembled, sip nog
Children cheerfully rip into the horde
Only to discover doom and dismay

It's Christmas, embargo be damned

New socks and underwear litter the floor
Scratchy sweaters we won't want to wear
Are all that Santa brought us that year

Christmas '73 be damned

Just More Journey

Flying forward, joyful
Expecting nothing, indelible

Time shifts, changes
Unexpected, unknown

Transgression? No
Don't ask questions, believe

Blind faith? Required
Enjoy the journey, tempting

Alteration? Definitely
To what end, what means

Smooth pavement, cracked
Determination, exhilaration

Pay the price, the bill
Blessings counted, move on

Reverse journey, not really
Forward momentum, still

Hurtling through time, space
Butte, knoll, quagmire, swamp

Destiny discovered, no
Never-ending life, bridge

Fish Gotta Swim

Glass box, journey contained
Light by day, and by night
No real rest, always moving

What thoughts drive us? What dreams?
Constantly churning, searching
Sustenance comes but once a day

Yet, still we search, with hope
Under that rock, this time, that sign
I meet you under the tree

Dusty air, filtered water
Paws occasionally intrude, pester
Great tormentor, randomly watching

And, still we swim, by day, by night
Beautiful searching, mating, not only
Surviving, but thriving

From Gregory...

Continued and ongoing thanks to Todd Isbell for your unending love.

I would like to extend my love and sincere thanks to Leslie E. Hoffman, Garry Buzick, Teresa L. Watts, Jan Lease, Douglas A. Davy, and Tena Beth Thompson, all members of the Laudably Tarnished Poetry Workshop, for their support, editing, companionship, and co-creation of a wonderful series of art experience.

The stories within many of these stanzas wouldn't have been possible without the life experiences that they reference. Some of you know who you are, others may not. Like the number of encounters, the co-creators of my life are virtually uncountable. So, to my family, friends, co-workers, and those I've shared chance meetings please accept my thanks and love.

About Gregory A. Kompes

Las Vegas Psychic Intuitive Gregory A. Kompes is the scribe for The Three Sisters. Learn more about this work at www.TheThreeSisters.net.

Gregory is the author of *Suddenly Psychic: Core Messages to Enhance your Psychic Journey, Message from The Three Sisters, Volumes 1, 2 & 3*, The Middleman, Flash Mob, First Dimension, and the bestselling *50 Fabulous Gay-Friendly Places to Live*. Gregory is also the author of the Writer's Series that includes: *Endorsement Quest, Creating Your Online Media Kit*, and *Should You Write an eBook*.

Additionally, the author is included in *Patchwork Path: Grandma's Choice, Patchwork Path: Dad's Bow Tie, Patchwork Path: Christmas Stoking, Patchwork Path: Treasure Box, Chicken Soup for the Soul: What I Learned from the Dog, Chopped Liver for the Kindred Spirit, Chopped Liver for the Gentle Spirit, The Complete Writer's Journal, Writer's Bloc: A Las Vegas Valley Authors' Showcase*, and *Writer's Bloc II*.

Gregory was co-founder of the Patchwork Path book series, co-host of the Writer's Pen and Grill, a social evening for writers held monthly in Las Vegas, Nevada, and co-founder of Laudably Tarnished: A Poetry Workshop.

Gregory holds a BA in English Literature from Columbia University, New York, a Certificate in Online Teaching and Learning, and an MS Ed. from California State University, East Bay.

Learn more and keep up with the latest at www.kompes.com